I
Will
Not Be Quiet
About It

Inspiring *spirit* to *Spirit* conversations
between *you* and *God.*

Brendal Bass Davis

Library of Congress Cataloging-in-Publication Data:

Davis, Brenda Bass

I will not be quiet about it / Brendal Bass Davis

ISBN: 978-1-7353210-6-6 (paperback)

LCCN: 2021937180

10 9 8 7 6 5 4 3 2 1

Printed in the United States of America

CONTENTS

ACKNOWLEDGMENTS

I am grateful to God for the deposits He made in me that have enabled me to write this Devotional Journal. The daily inspiration I receive from Him is unsurpassed. To Him, I give glory.

To my beloved daughter, Dr. Trellis Davis, this happened because you strengthened me. You gave me a jump start by inviting me to join your writers' group. Your love, prayers, patience, and encouragement inspired me to finish what I started. Thank you for believing in mama and the inspirational value of my life experiences.

To Bishop Kirby Clements, thank you for your encouraging words over the years. When you told me to write books and booklets, I was confident that I heard from God through you. I will forever trust the God in you, sir.

To Bishop Frederick Nah, Jr., after seeing me twice, you spoke into my life. Thank you for your words of encouragement to write "books." Your words were a confirmation.

To Pastor James Powers and the Motivators Prayer Group, we have been together for over 34 years. Thank you for your unconditional love and support over the years. To Willie E. (Dave) Davis, our founder, and my late husband, thank you for what you pressed out of me and for the investments you made in me. I can imagine you saying to God, "one out and more to come." And to me, "get busy, mama."

To Gerald, my husband, thank you. Your unconscious influence on me to see beyond daily challenges to where God is taking me is empowering. I will not quit; I will stay with God.

Thank you for your professionalism, attention, and understanding of the purpose of this project to the dedicated team at Tandem Light Press.

I dedicate this devotional journal to my daddy, Wallace Henry Bass. For as long as I can remember, my daddy enjoyed "Talking to the Lord," and I knew it. How did I know?

I knew because he was not quiet about it.

I would often fall asleep while riding with him and wake up in the middle of his conversation with the Lord.

He was not quiet about it.

When I visited him at the Presbyterian Home, I walked into the room and he was facing the wall praying. When I asked, "Daddy, what are you doing?" he said, "Talking to the Lord."

He was not quiet about it.

At home, in church, in the car, in the yard, when my dad was alone with God praying, I heard him. Silently praying under his breath was not his thing. And I saw him praying; even when I did not hear a sound, I knew by looking at him that he was praying. His actions were loud and clear: he was on speaking terms with God.

He was not quiet about it.

Daddy, I learned about conversations with God from the best—you—and

I will not be quiet about it.

INTRODUCTION

My beloved Aunt Thelma made friendship cakes for sharing with family and friends. It was an act of love for Auntie. First, she made what is called a starter. Every day for approximately sixty days, the starter was in process. At the end of the process, she had starters to share with those who wanted to make a friendship cake themselves, and she had cakes to share with those who just wanted to enjoy eating her friendship cake.

Like Aunt Thelma's friendship cake starters, the devotionals in this book can help start your time of prayer and meditation with the Lord, or they can be used word for word. Either way, whenever you boldly approach God's throne to commune with Him, be who *you* are and communicate in your unique style. When you talk with Him, know that He is listening to your heart and your voice.

Know that God hears and answers prayers, and whether we like His timing and answers or not, God is always on time and His answers are still right.

"When you call on me, when you come and pray to me, I'll listen."

Jeremiah 29:12 The Message (MSG)

As you adopt these devotionals, I hope they will strengthen your relationship with God and build confidence in who you are. Believe in your ability to hear from God as you say prayers of faith; you will get results. Don't be quiet about it!

LIVING WITH PASSION

Christian living is not perfect living. Yes, abundant life, peaceful living, joyful living, healthy living, and prosperous living are a part of God's master plan for His children.

And yes, Christian living is a balancing act. There will be sunshine and rain; expect it. There will be joy and pain; expect it. The blessing is, Christ saves you from drowning in the (rain) storms of life, and He saves you from getting stuck in (the pain and) grief you will experience in life.

Ultimately, abundant living goes beyond fortune and fame. It is not about the car you drive or the house you live in, or the clothes you may or may not be able to afford. It has nothing to do with your level of education. It is, first and foremost, the gift of salvation. And then it is about the Kingdom of God—righteousness, peace, and joy in the Holy Ghost. Righteous living gives you peace, and peace brings joy—all compliments of the Holy Spirit.

Are you saved? Are you a citizen of God's Kingdom, with entitlement to His promises? Do you know who you are, your purpose in life? If your answer is yes to these questions, you are a candidate for abundant life and the challenges that come with it. The good news is: Life is worth living because Jesus came so that you might have an abundant life; so focus on and enjoy living this kind of life. Then God will be glorified, and you will be satisfied.

Are you passionate about life, your life, the life God gave you?

Living with Passion: Listen to what the Spirit says about it, and record what you hear.

_____

_____

_____

_____

_____

_____

_____

_____

_____

_____

_____

_____

_____

_____

_____

_____

_____

_____

Date: _____

LIFE'S DIVINE ORDER

"So God created human beings in his own image. In the image of God he created them; male and female he created them. Then God blessed them and said, 'Be fruitful and multiply. Fill the earth and govern it. Reign over the fish in the sea, the birds in the sky, and all the animals that scurry along the ground.' Then God said, 'Look! I have given you every seed-bearing plant throughout the earth and all the fruit trees for your food.'"

GENESIS 1:27–29 (NIV)

IS THERE ANYTHING in life outside of being, doing, and having? One of the most powerful lessons we can learn and teach our children is *divine order*. Life is about Being, Doing, and Having. Without knowing and being who we were born to be, and without knowing and doing what we were created and gifted to do, unfulfillment, lack of direction, and frustration are probable. According to Genesis 1:29, the Bible tells us that when our life is in order (being, then doing), then God said "Look! I have given you..." There is great joy in knowing that when we are in divine order, what we desire, God has already given. It is in being fruitful and multiplying that God is enabling you to have the desires of your life. When a giver gives, God gives back. If you are a singer, sing, and your singing will bring God glory and you the desires of your heart.

❦

Prayer Focus: Divine order

Prayer Starter: Almighty God. You are my Creator, the one who created me to be who I am and the one who gifted me to do what I am doing. Lord, I want to live life in divine order and bring you glory. Thank you for the manifestation of everything you have given me

_____

_____

_____

_____

_____

_____

_____

_____

In Jesus' name I pray. Amen, amen, and amen!

❧

Is your life in divine order? Is your focus on being who you were born to be and doing what your God created you to do, so you can have the abundant life Jesus came for you to have?

Life's Divine Order: Listen to what the Spirit says about it, and record what you hear.

_____

_____

_____

_____

_____

_____

_____

_____

_____

_____

_____

_____

_____

_____

_____

_____

_____

_____

_____

_____

_____

Date: _____

THE RIGHT FOCUS AND THE RIGHT MEASURE OF SUCCESS

"Many are the plans in a person's heart, but it is the Lord's purpose that prevails."

Proverbs 19:21 (NIV)

I READ A story some years ago about a man named Mr. Chambers. Mr. Chambers was a success by worldly standards. His parents were proud of who he had become, his wife had everything she could ever want and was happy, his children were well educated and working in his businesses, and his bank accounts were full. Still, because he was unfulfilled, he attempted to take his life. Mr. Chambers' words to the young admirer who saved him from an attempted suicide were life-changing: "Do not try to be like me; find out who you are, and *be yourself.*"

᪐

Prayer Focus: Be who you are, *not* who you want to be unless who you want to be is who you were born to be.

Prayer Starter: Almighty God, my Maker and Creator, I am Your child and You know all about me. I am grateful that You have already determined my destiny. Now Lord, I ask that You reveal me to me: my natural and spiritual gifts, my strengths and weaknesses, the condition of my heart. Reveal the me You created me to be and fill my heart with the desire to be me. My choice is for the fulfillment of Your plans and purpose for my life. Enable me now by the power of the Holy Spirit to maintain the right focus and the right measure so that I can bring You glory

_____

_____

_____

_____

_____

_____

_____

In Jesus' name I pray. Amen, amen, and amen!

ॐ

Is success your primary life focus? How do you measure success?

WHEN YOU WANT TO KNOW "WHAT'S NEXT"

"Trust God from the bottom of your heart;
   don't try to figure out everything on your own.
Listen for God's voice in everything you do, everywhere you go;
   he's the one who will keep you on track."

PROVERBS 3:5–6 (MSG)

Graduation was quickly approaching, and I did not have a clue about my "what's next," but what I did have was a relationship with God, the One who knew my "what's next" and how He was going to get me there. Sitting in the middle of my bed with my hymn book open to the song "Sweet Hour of Prayer," I called on Him, I went to Him, and I prayed as I had never prayed before. "Almighty God," I said, "My future looks so dark. What am I going to do after graduation?" He was listening, and almost straightaway, He answered. In what seemed like an instant, my high school counselor, Mrs. Margaret McIver, called me to her office and said, "Bass, you are going to Morris Brown College in Atlanta." I did not ask one question because I knew in my spirit that it was the answer to my prayer. God was directing my path to my "next." Morris Brown was the only college to which I applied. God was listening when I was thinking; He answered when I opened my mouth and asked Him. In August 1968, I enrolled in Morris Brown College on scholarships and loans. Like my daddy, I was not quiet about it.

❧

Prayer Focus: Trusting God wholeheartedly

Prayer Starter: All-Knowing God, You knew my end before my beginning. Your Word says that You will keep my life on track if I trust You and not my understanding. God, I trust You wholeheartedly. My spiritual antenna is up, my ears are open and listening, so I ask that You speak to me about my future about the path You have set before me

_____

_____

_____

_____

_____

_____

_____

In Jesus' name I pray. Amen, amen, and amen!

◈

Are you wondering how your life will play out? Are you trusting God or are you trying to figure it out yourself?

When you want to know "what's next," listen to what the Spirit says about it and record what you hear.

_____

_____

_____

_____

_____

_____

_____

_____

_____

_____

_____

_____

_____

_____

_____

_____

_____

_____

_____

_____

_____

_____

Date: _____

KEEP MOVING!

"When you go through deep waters, I will be with you.
When you go through rivers of difficulty, you will not drown.
When you walk through the fire of oppression, you will not
be burned up; the flames will not consume you."

Isaiah 43:2 (NLT)

There are situations in your life from which you feel like you can
never heal. The trauma that they cause may make it challenging to
bounce back. I was at these crossroads too. What do you do when
you go from happily married to being a widow? What do you do
when experiencing the shame of divorce when you do not believe
in divorce? What do you do when you are oppressed or depressed
by the possibility of losing your only child? What do you do when
you experience for the first time in your life how jealousy that is
cruel as a grave feels? As I faced these situations and circumstances,
I knew they were beyond my capacity to handle them. No matter
how much of a Christian you are, *alone,* you cannot survive in
deep waters forever, you cannot survive rivers of difficulty indefi-
nitely, you cannot withstand the fire of oppression but for so long.
I needed to know I could make it. The Word of God in Isaiah 43:2
assured me that I was not alone, and with God, I could *keep moving.*
Are you stuck in a situation or circumstance causing you to wonder
if you can make it through? Stand on the Word in Isaiah 43:2 and
do not stop; *keep moving.* You are not alone.

❦

Prayer Focus: Survival

Prayer Starter: Oh Lord, my God, my Savior, there is nothing too hard for You. You are the God who is with me in the sunshine and the rain, in joy and pain. Even when I am not good, you remain great. Thank You for Your presence in my life and for enabling me to press on when I am tempted to give up. Thank You, Lord for giving me a way of escape when it seems the enemy is consuming my mind

_____

_____

_____

_____

_____

_____

_____

In Jesus' name I pray. Amen, amen, and amen!

✆

Are you questioning how you are going to make it through? Do you realize that you are never alone?

Keep Moving: Listen to what the Spirit says about it, and record what you hear.

_____

_____

_____

_____

_____

_____

_____

_____

_____

_____

_____

_____

_____

_____

_____

_____

_____

_____

_____

_____

_____

_____

Date: _____

TWO YEAR TRIAL

"Consider it a sheer gift, friends, when tests and challenges come at you from all sides. You know that under pressure, your faith-life is forced into the open and shows its true colors. So don't try to get out of anything prematurely. Let it do its work so you become mature and well-developed, not deficient in any way."

James 1:2–4 (MSG)

I was anxious. Things were moving too slowly. I need to sell these rental properties because they were getting on my last nerve, and I just did not want to do it anymore. I prayed, and it seemed like God did not care, but He did. On August 29, 2017, James 1:3 made it crystal clear and I recorded in my prayer journal, "Know this, Brendal, that the trying of your faith worketh patience." Like it or not, my faith was on trial. I had to be patient and wait. On August 26, 2019, that piece of property sold for twice as much as I had been willing to sell it for two years earlier. When my faith kicked in, my anxiety turned to patience, and my patience brought me more than I initially asked. When you get anxious and wonder where God is, stand on James 1:3, knowing that by faith, you can go through your trials patiently, and your patience may bring you more than you initially expected.

⁂

Prayer Focus: Faith on trial

Prayer Starter: Our God, our help in ages past, our hope for years to come. Thank You for the trials that build my faith, and thank You for the gift of faith that yields the fruit of patience. Thank You for enabling me to see You at work in all things pertaining to my life…

_____

_____

_____

_____

_____

_____

_____

_____

In Jesus' name I pray. Amen, amen, and amen!

∽

Do you believe delay does not mean denial in the Kingdom of God? Have you accepted the fact that it is all about God's timing?

Two Year Trial: Listen to what the Spirit says about it, and record what you hear.

_____

_____

_____

_____

_____

_____

_____

_____

_____

_____

_____

_____

_____

_____

_____

_____

_____

_____

_____

_____

_____

Date: _____

SEEING BEYOND THE ORDINARY

"By your words, I can see where I'm going;
they throw a beam of light on my dark path."

PSALM 119:105 (MSG)

HAVE YOU EVER been in a dark place? When I left home for work on November 18, 1991, I was a happily married mother. When I returned home from work, I was a forty-year-old widow and single mother with a seventeen-year-old daughter, a senior in high school, to educate. It felt as if my security blanket was ripped off. For the first time in twenty years, I was in a place of uncertainty and wondering, "Where am I and where am I going?" One of the things that helped me see beyond the darkness and uncertainty of my future were the words to the song "Order My Steps in Your Word." The lyrics to that song took up residence in my spirit. I hummed those words over and over again. "Order my steps in Your Word, dear Lord. Lead me, guide me every day. Send your anointing, Father, I pray. Order my steps in Your Word." Then it started happening; I began seeing beyond the darkness of where I was, the darkness of fear of failure and being alone, and beyond the everyday routine. I started seeing the light of the path God set before me, and it was not ordinary. A way paved with purpose, the direction where fear of failure faded in the light of power, love, and a sound mind. The Word of God enabled me to see beyond the ordinary. Glory to God.

Prayer Focus: God's Word

Prayer Starter: Thank You, Lord, for guiding me with Your Word. You are the Way and I am grateful because I can see beyond the ordinary. I can see where I am and where I am going because of the beam of light in Your Word that directs my path

_____

_____

_____

_____

_____

_____

_____

_____

In Jesus' name I pray. Amen, amen, and amen!

✎

Are you wondering what lies ahead in your life? Ever wished you could see what tomorrow holds?

Seeing beyond the ordinary: Listen to what the Spirit says about it, and record what you hear.

_____

_____

_____

_____

_____

_____

_____

_____

_____

_____

_____

_____

_____

_____

_____

_____

_____

_____

_____

_____

Date: _____

REST

"The apostles then rendezvoused with Jesus and reported on all that they had done and taught. Jesus said, 'Come off by yourselves; let's take a break and get a little rest.' For there was constant coming and going. They didn't even have time to eat."

MARK 6:30–31 (MSG)

GROWING UP, TAKING naps was not the norm in our household. But when you were sick, or it was raining or thundering and lightning outside, it was expected. After doing chores, you were supposed to play or do your homework. My parents did not take naps or simply rest. There was always something to do. When they finished, they went to bed for a "good night's sleep."

After getting remarried in 2010, I had to adjust to my husband taking a nap every day after returning home from work. Not only did he take a nap, but he also insisted that I needed to take naps. Please do not judge me, but I thought it was a sin until I read and accepted the advice Jesus gave the Apostles in Mark 6:30–31: "Get a little rest."

Are you like the apostles coming and going and not even taking time to rest or eat properly? If so, take Jesus' advice, take a break, and get a little rest. It is refreshing, mentally, spiritually, and physically.

❧

Prayer Focus: Taking care of your temple

Prayer Starter: All-wise God, Creator of all things. Thank You for giving me the wisdom to know how to take care of my temple. The wisdom to know when to go and know when to stay. The wisdom to know when to say yes and to know when to say no. Thank you for giving me rest

_____

_____

_____

_____

_____

_____

_____

_____

In Jesus' name I pray. Amen, amen, and amen!

✍

Is "busy" your soft addiction? Are you always on the go and wondering where did the time go? Do you avoid saying, "I am tired?"

Rest: Listen to what the Spirit says about it, and record what you hear.

_____

_____

_____

_____

_____

_____

_____

_____

_____

_____

_____

_____

_____

_____

_____

_____

_____

_____

_____

_____

Date: _____

CROSSROADS

"Trust in the Lord with all your heart,
And lean not on your own understanding;
In all your ways acknowledge Him,
And He shall direct your paths."

PROVERBS 3:5–6 (NKJV)

WHAT DO YOU do when you are standing at a crossroads in your life, wondering what path to take? When I was a teenager, my grandmother Helen, who we called Mama, prepared me for my most challenging times when she told me what to do.

We were a deacon team, Dave and me. As ordained deacons, we were responsible for one of the largest deacons' groups in our megachurch. He was a natural motivator who people loved to follow. And then, November 18, 1991, he left for his Heavenly home as a result of a fishing accident, and there I was standing at the crossroad of my deacon's ministry, asking God, "Where do I go from here? Do I keep serving the group, or do I step aside?" God's answer was instant and precise: "Follow Me." When I told my pastor I would continue serving, he was not surprised, and not once did he question my ability to care for the people.

Mama's life lesson was simple: When you find yourself at a crossroads in life, "fall on your knees and ask God, where do I go from here?"

❧

Prayer Focus: Directions from God

Prayer Starter: Omnipotent, Omniscient, Omnipresent God, thank You for Your presence in my life. In the hard places, You are there; in the areas of uncertainty and not knowing, You are there. Thank You for meeting me at the crossroads of my life and giving me direction, protection, peace, and the desire to follow You

_____

_____

_____

_____

_____

_____

_____

In Jesus' name I pray. Amen, amen, and amen!

∽

Are you wondering which way to go? Not sure which option is the right one?

Crossroads: Listen to what the Spirit says about it, and record what you hear.

_____

_____

_____

_____

_____

_____

_____

_____

_____

_____

_____

_____

_____

_____

_____

_____

_____

_____

_____

Date: _____

PREVAILING

"We humans keep brainstorming options and plans, but
God's purpose prevails."

PROVERBS 19:21 (MSG)

I HAVE OFTEN wondered how did I get here, or how did I make
it, or how did I overcome it. The truth is: I have always known.
However, while I was going through it, I was not present with
that truth. My favorite scripture says it all. I was prevailing because
of God's purpose for my life.

As a single woman, I was prevailing. As a married woman, I was
prevailing. It was hard, painful, lonely, and unbelievable as a widow,
but I was prevailing. When I married again, I was prevailing. As a
divorcee, dealing with shame and disappointment, I was prevailing.
I have remarried, and I know that God's purpose for my life is still
prevailing.

Because Christ strengthens me, and because the Holy Spirit
guides me, I can do all the things I have to do for God's purpose to
prevail in my life.

❧

Prayer Focus: God's prevailing purpose

Prayer Starter: Almighty King, You, are my enabler. You are the Way. Even when I do not know what I need to know, You, Lord, understand, and by the guidance of the Holy Spirit, You guide me. Forgive me when I hesitate because I am walking by sight. Thank You for Your purpose for my life. Thank You for the desire and passion You have given me to fulfill Your purpose for my life

_____

_____

_____

_____

_____

_____

_____

In Jesus' name I pray. Amen, amen, and amen!

⮥

Do you know that God's purpose for your life is unstoppable? Are you aware that God's purpose is better than the best plan you will ever develop? And that He is the One who, through your obedience, will fulfill His purpose?

Prevailing: Listen to what the Spirit says about it, and record what you hear.

_____

_____

_____

_____

_____

_____

_____

_____

_____

_____

_____

_____

_____

_____

_____

_____

_____

_____

Date: _____

HEART VISION

"I pray that the eyes of your heart may be enlightened in order that you may know the hope to which he has called you, the riches of his glorious inheritance in his holy people."

EPHESIANS 1:18 (NIV)

THE TONGUE IS dangerous, but undoubtedly, the heart is the most powerful and vital part of the body. When the heart stops beating, life ends.

Although the Ephesians' faith was growing and they were abounding in love, Paul asked the Lord to open the eyes of their hearts so that they, like Isaiah, could see the Lord "high and lifted" and they would be discerning and intelligent.

It is by the power of the Holy Spirit that our hearts are open so we can see forgiveness through the fog of unforgiveness. Heart vision is faith-based; it is discerning; it enables us to see people's true nature. Heart vision allows us to see below the surface. The question is, what do you see through the eyes of your heart? When dealing with the situations and circumstances of life, what do you see? Do you see forgiveness for those who offend you? With heart vision, you can.

❧

Prayer Focus: Seeing with the eyes of your heart

Prayer Starter: God of glory, Giver of every good and perfect gift, thank You for a discerning spirit. Thank You for opening the eyes of my heart, so I can see and experience You as a Forgiver, Lover, Savior, Healer, a Deliverer, as Peace, and as a Provider. Thank You

_____

_____

_____

_____

_____

_____

_____

In Jesus' name I pray. Amen, amen, and amen!

&

Are the eyes of your heart open? Are you discerning?

Heart vision: Listen to what the Spirit says about it, and record what you hear.

_____

_____

_____

_____

_____

_____

_____

_____

_____

_____

_____

_____

_____

_____

_____

_____

_____

_____

_____

_____

_____

_____

Date: _____

THE SECURE PLACE

"Father, into Your hands I commit my spirit."

Luke 23:46 (NIV)

WHEN GROWING UP in my father's house, turnkey was an unfamiliar term. There was no key, and we had not heard of a security system. Things have changed; not only are people locking their doors, but they are also installing security systems with cameras that record and store recordings in the cloud. All to make their homes safe and secure. Still, there are break-ins and home invasions every day, and it is difficult for us, at best, to identify a secure place.

The good news is that while hanging on the cross at Calvary, Jesus identified the place where we can find security that cannot be compromised. Even if your home has a security system, take a cue from Jesus, and put your life in the secure place of the Father's hands.

Although we did not have a lock on our doors when I was growing up, my earthly father secured our family by putting us in the secure place of our Heavenly Father's hands. Is your life in the safety of the Father's hands?

≪

Prayer Focus: Security in the hands of God

Prayer Starter: Omnipotent and Omniscient God, we are weak, but You are mighty. We ask that You hold us in the hollow of Your hands. Put a hedge of protection around us. Protect us from all hurt, harm, and danger

_____

_____

_____

_____

_____

_____

_____

In Jesus' name I pray. Amen, amen, and amen!

∽

Is security important to you? Where is the safest place one can be? Are you dwelling in that place?

The Secure Place: Listen to what the Spirit says about it, and record what you hear.

_____

_____

_____

_____

_____

_____

_____

_____

_____

_____

_____

_____

_____

_____

_____

_____

_____

_____

_____

_____

Date: _____

STANDING

"Heaven and earth will pass away, but My words will by no means pass away."

Matthew 24:35 (NKJV)

VISITATION—WITH THE SICK and well—is a faith-building experience. It is also an opportunity to inspire and encourage people to remember who they can always depend on in good times and challenging times. After listening and before I pray with them, I ask a standard question, "Where are you standing?" Most wonder what I am talking about, while others are quick to say, "I'm standing on the Word." And then I ask, "On what Word are you standing?" The sick are encouraged to stand on the Word that says, "By His stripes, they are healed." When they have a need, I encourage them to stand on the Word, "God shall supply all of your needs according to His riches in glory by Christ Jesus." Those who need peace are encouraged to stand on the Word that says, "Do not worry. Pray, thank God for His answers, and He will give you peace that passes all understanding."

No matter what your need is today, by faith, I encourage you to focus on "standing" on the promises—the Word—of God.

∽

Prayer Focus: Standing on the promises of God—His Word.

Prayer Starter: Almighty God, You are Your word and You never fail. Thank You for Your unfailing promises. I come today declaring my faith in You. God, I ask that, in accordance with Your Word, You will

_____

_____

_____

_____

_____

_____

_____

In Jesus' name I pray. Amen, amen, and amen!

❧

Are you positioned to receive what God has for you? Are you standing on the promises of God?

Standing: Listen to what the Spirit says about it, and record what you hear.

_____

_____

_____

_____

_____

_____

_____

_____

_____

_____

_____

_____

_____

_____

_____

_____

_____

_____

_____

_____

Date: _____

WHEN ESCORTED BY THE HELP

"I will lift up my eyes to the hills—
From whence comes my help?
My help comes from the Lord,
Who made heaven and earth."

PSALM 121:1–2 (NKJV)

ONE OF THE Songs of Ascent pilgrims would sing as they traveled to Jerusalem for an annual feast is Psalms 121. Unlike today, there were no gospel stations that they could listen to for inspiration as they went. These Songs of Accent were their inspiration.

In Dr. Martin Luther King's words, the Psalmist knew that there were "some difficult days ahead," as they traveled paths where there were real and imagined dangers. Knowing what was ahead, he inspired those traveling to focus on Who would escort them to Jerusalem.

We are all on a journey called life. Our experiences on this journey may be different; the paths we take will be different. Although our lives are ever-changing, our tours continue, and we will make it alright if we know and acknowledge the Lord as our escort, who is the Help we need.

❦

Prayer Focus: The Lord, our Escort, and the Help we need.

Prayer Starter: Oh Lord God, You, are the Help I need when the road is rough. You alone have the power to make rough places smooth and crooked places straight. I know I cannot make it without You. Holy Spirit, You are my guide. I ask that You walk with me, lead, guide, direct, and protect me. Escort me, Lord, on this journey called life. I pray

_____

_____

_____

_____

_____

_____

_____

In the matchless name of Jesus I pray. Amen, amen and amen.

❧

Do you need someone to accompany you on your life's journey? Who are you looking to for direction and protection?

When escorted by the Help: Listen to what the Spirit says about it, and record what you hear.

_____

_____

_____

_____

_____

_____

_____

_____

_____

_____

_____

_____

_____

_____

_____

_____

_____

_____

_____

_____

_____

Date: _____

ONLY THE STRONG SURVIVES

"Have I not commanded you? Be strong and courageous.
Do not be afraid; do not be discouraged, for the Lord your
God will be with you wherever you go."

JOSHUA 1:9 (NIV)

I T IS NOT a suggestion; it is a command. It is not either–or; it
is both "strong" and "courageous."

Some years ago, my brother, Adolphus, came to my rescue
and left me with these words: "Only the strong survive." Since
then, I have learned through life experiences that being strong is
not always enough; it also takes courage.

It took strength and courage for little David to challenge and
prevail against Goliath. It took strength and courage for Esther to
expose Haman and save her people. Have you, or someone you
know, been in a situation where you had the strength (power) to act
but not the courage to use that power? It happens. Some people have
the strength or advantage of their God-given vision, gifts, talents,
and resources to start a business, write a book, create a product, but
they lack the courage to do it. The strong and courageous not only
survive, but they also succeed and thrive. Why? Because "the Lord
your God will be with you wherever you go" or whatever you do.
When God is ordering your steps, failure is just a stepping stone on
your pathway to success. God's got you: Be strong and courageous."

≪

Prayer Focus: Strength and courage

Prayer Starter: Heavenly Father, thank you for the plans you have for my life. Holy Spirit, order my steps as I move forward with strength and courage to reach my full potential and as I face the many challenges in life

_____

_____

_____

_____

_____

_____

_____

In Jesus' name I pray. Amen, amen, and amen!

✌

What is your strategy for survival? What do you need to keep moving forward?

Only the strong survive: Listen to what the Spirit says about it, and record what you hear.

_____

_____

_____

_____

_____

_____

_____

_____

_____

_____

_____

_____

_____

_____

_____

_____

_____

_____

_____

_____

_____

Date: _____

OVERCOMING SHAME

"For the Lord God helps me,
Therefore, I have not been ashamed or humiliated.
Therefore, I have made my face like flint,
And I know that I shall not be put to shame."

Isaiah 50:7 Amplified Bible (AMP)

I WAS ASHAMED of myself. I, the leader of a Covenant Community Group, a deacon, prayer group leader, and although it was not intentional, I had become a role model for some. Above all, I was born to be a wife and mother. How was I going to tell everyone that I was divorced? I did not believe in divorce, but I was divorced and ashamed! How do you move on when gripped with the fear of embarrassment and failure?

First, embrace the reality of who you are and whose you are. Knowing you are a Christian, a child of God, is the game-changer because it gives you the strength and courage to do what you must do. Secondly, acknowledge that fear of failure and other people's opinions are the sources of your embarrassment and shame.

Then, remember, you are never alone. The Lord, the Forgiver, was with me; my pastor believed in and supported me. My family, covenant community, and real friends loved and respected me. I was not alone and not powerless. The shame had to go.

Be encouraged; shame is something you can overcome. Remember, "There is now no condemnation for those who are in Christ Jesus." Believe it!

❧

Prayer Focus Overcoming shame

Prayer Starter: Almighty God, there are times when I forget who I am and whose I am. Holy Spirit, help me always to remember that it is more important to please God than man and that I am never alone in any situation or circumstance

_____

_____

_____

_____

_____

_____

_____

In Jesus' name I pray. Amen, amen, and amen!

∽

Have you ever been ashamed of yourself? Have you thought to yourself, why did I do that or I do not believe I did that?

Overcoming shame: Listen to what the Spirit says about it, and record what you hear.

_____

_____

_____

_____

_____

_____

_____

_____

_____

_____

_____

_____

_____

_____

_____

_____

_____

_____

_____

_____

Date: _____

EQUIPPED FOR SUCCESS

"When it came to presenting the Message to people who had no background in God's way, I was the least qualified of any of the available Christians. God saw to it that I was equipped, but you can be sure that it had nothing to do with my natural abilities."

EPHESIANS 3:8 (MSG)

PAUL MADE IT clear that God equipped him to preach the gospel of Jesus Christ, and he had nothing to do with it. Like Paul, God armed you for success. God provided everything—spiritual and natural gifts, talent, His divine essence, the whole armor of Jesus Christ, the fruit of the Holy Spirit, wisdom—yes, everything needed for His people to live an abundant life, a successful life.

Whatever you are equipped to do—teach, sing, dance, cook, encourage, serve others, provide leadership—do it with a spirit of excellence. God's design and purpose for your life is a done deal, completed. Now it is the time for you to bring Him glory by doing what Paul did. Acknowledge that God equipped you, confidently use what God provided, and succeed.

❦

Prayer Focus: Equipped to live life

Prayer Starter: Creator of Heaven and Earth; omnipotent, omniscient God, thank you for all you have invested in me. On the authority of Your Word and by the power of the Holy Spirit, I declare I will live an abundant life. I am Your child. I am full of purpose. I have Your joy that gives me strength. I have natural and spiritual gifts. I thank you for every good and perfect gift

_____

_____

_____

_____

_____

_____

In Jesus' name I pray. Amen, amen, and amen!

∽

What are you equipped to do? Where did your equipment come from—God or man? Can you take the credit?

Equipped for success: Listen to what the Spirit says about it, and record what you hear.

_____

_____

_____

_____

_____

_____

_____

_____

_____

_____

_____

_____

_____

_____

_____

_____

_____

_____

_____

_____

Date: _____

I 💡 THINK

"How could he? For certainly he has never been one to
know the Lord's thoughts, or to discuss them with him,
or to move the hands of God by prayer. But, strange as it
seems, we Christians actually do have within us a portion of
the very thoughts and mind of Christ."

1 CORINTHIANS 2:16 (LIVING)

THINK ABOUT IT: Christians have within them "a portion
of the very thoughts and mind of Christ." This scripture
should make us more aware of what we say following the
words "I think." Are our thoughts influenced or guided by His
thoughts?

Some years ago, I taught a class entitled "What's on Your Mind?"
to a group of Fulton County parolees. My message was, if you think
the right thoughts, you will say good things, and you will do the
right things.

During the 2020 Pandemic, organizations, including the
church, are re-thinking how they do business or operate. With individuals, including Christians, it is about what iThink because I have
the "very thoughts and mind of Christ"; what iThink is essential.

෴

Prayer Focus: Thinking like Jesus

Prayer Starter: Most Gracious Heavenly Father, thank You for giving me the mind of Christ that enables me to declare, iThink as He thinks. God, iThink it is more important to obey You than man; iThink it is more blessed to give than to receive; iThink I must forgive if I want to be forgiven

_____

_____

_____

_____

_____

_____

_____

_____

In Jesus' name I pray. Amen, amen, and amen!

❧

From where did that thought come? Who influences your train of thought?

I 💡 **think: Listen to what the Spirit says about it, and record what you hear.**

_____

_____

_____

_____

_____

_____

_____

_____

_____

_____

_____

_____

_____

_____

_____

_____

_____

_____

_____

_____

_____

_____

_____

Date: _____

LOVING UNCONDITIONALLY

"Dear children, let us not love with words or speech but with actions and in truth."

1 JOHN 3:18 (NIV)

"Don't just pretend that you love others: really love them. Hate what is wrong. Stand on the side of the good. Love each other with brotherly affection and take delight in honoring each other."

ROMANS 12:9–10 (LIVING)

MY GRANDMOTHER, HELEN, who we called Mama, taught us many lessons, and one I will always remember is: "Love is what you do." Rarely did they quote chapter and verse from the Bible when I was growing up. More importantly, they lived the Bible. As I was growing up, I did not hear the words "I love you" regularly. But every day, I knew I was loved, and every day I felt the love of my village. How did I know it? What made me feel like it? It was what they did.

As I matured, I learned that Mama was right; not only did I experience love in action, personally, God blessed me to see my village practice what they preached when they said, "Love everybody."

Can you imagine life without the love of God and man? I do not want to even think about it. I need both. If you need it, give it. Loving is healing. Loving is a powerful way of living.

Are you experiencing love in action? Are you demonstrating love through your actions? Love is a beautiful thing for the giver and the receiver.

Loving Unconditionally: Listen to what the Spirit says about it, and record what you hear.

_____

_____

_____

_____

_____

_____

_____

_____

_____

_____

_____

_____

_____

_____

_____

_____

_____

_____

_____

_____

Date: _____

LOVE NEVER QUITS

"Thank God because he's good, because his love never quits. Tell the world, Israel, 'His love never quits.' And you, clan of Aaron, tell the world, 'His love never quits.' And you who fear God, join in, 'His love never quits.'"

PSALM 118:1–4 (MSG)

A YOUNG LADY called our prayer line, asking for prayer because she believed God no longer loved her because of something she did. I heard the fear in her voice. There are times when it may be challenging to bring calm to a situation when a person's fear of God is intense. This prayer request was one of those challenging times. I had a "me first" moment. First, before I could pray for her, I had to pray for myself quickly. As I listened to her, my first thought was, *You should be afraid; I would be.* I quickly realized that I was judging the lady and needed the Holy Spirit to help me get beyond the shock of what she had done to the point of sharing with her the One Who had the power of forgiveness in this situation.

After listening to her story, God-vision enabled me to see through what she confessed to the truth that "His love never quits." Yes, we all reap what we sow, and the reaping may be hard to bear; but because God is a good God, a forgiving God, and because God is love, He will never quit loving.

It took a moment for tears to cease and to calm her fears, but there is nothing too hard for the Omnipotent God whose love never quits.

Be encouraged, no matter what you have done or ever will do; no matter what people say or how they judge you, God will always love you.

꿍

Prayer Focus: The love of God

Prayer Starter: Father, You are a great God who is good to me. You are the God who has the power to forgive me my sins and transgressions. Thank you for the peace in knowing that not only will you forgive me but that you will never quit loving me

_____

_____

_____

_____

_____

_____

_____

In Jesus' name I pray. Amen, amen, and amen!

∽

Can you imagine what life would be like without the love of God? Can you make it without it?

Love never quits: Listen to what the Spirit says about it, and record what you hear.

_____

_____

_____

_____

_____

_____

_____

_____

_____

_____

_____

_____

_____

_____

_____

_____

_____

_____

_____

Date: _____

FAVOR: ALL GOD

"But let all who take refuge in you be glad;
   let them ever sing for joy.
Spread your protection over them,
   that those who love your name may rejoice in you.
Surely, Lord, you bless the righteous;
   you surround them with your favor as with a shield."

PSALM 5:11–12 (NIV)

YOU ARE ONE of many applicants for your dream job, and from your perspective, some are more qualified than you. Then you get the call offering you the job, your dream job. You are overjoyed, yet wondering how you got selected. Maybe it was not a job; it was a house, a car, a business opportunity. No matter what it was, there is no need to wonder because the Psalmist provided the answer. It was all God, His favor, that gave you the advantage, the victory.

When you put your trust in Him and live according to His will and purpose for your life, God protects you and everything concerning you. Pray without ceasing, trust Him, and sing for joy, expecting Him to surround you with His favor as with a shield; a shield no man can penetrate.

᪥

Prayer Focus: God's favor

Prayer Starter: Most Gracious Heavenly Father, You are awesome in all your ways. You are the One I can trust in all things. You are the God who has the power to favor me even in my uncertainty. For that and more, God, I say thank You. I am grateful for what You have already done for me. I pray for the wisdom to know how to behave when You favor me. May I always be aware that You bless me to be a blessing to others in a way that You get the glory.

_____

_____

_____

_____

_____

_____

_____

In Jesus' name I pray. Amen, amen, and amen!

⁊

Have you ever experienced the favor of God? Did it blow your mind to see the possible in the impossible?

Favor: All God. Listen to what the Spirit says about it, and record what you hear.

_____

_____

_____

_____

_____

_____

_____

_____

_____

_____

_____

_____

_____

_____

_____

_____

_____

Date: _____

GIVE WHO YOU ARE

"For this is how God loved the world: He gave his one and only Son, so that everyone who believes in him will not perish but have eternal life."

JOHN 3:16 (NLT)

THE FIRST SERMON I wrote for Dr. Davis' class when attending Luther Rice Seminary was entitled "Give Who You Are." It was a Christmas message inspired by the text and a statement I had recently heard: "The greatest gift you can give your children is the gift of who you are." I struggled to limit that sermon to the required doubled spaced five pages because my life experiences were full of examples. My earthly father and mother gave us who they were, empowering us to love in the face of hate, survive on the many God-given gifts they helped us develop, and use our senses with wisdom. God created His children in His image, love, and He gave us Jesus, love, the greatest gift He could give. He gave us who He is, and we must do the same thing. Give generously the gift of who you are so that God gets the glory, you get satisfaction, and the people you inspire experience gratification.

 తా

Prayer Focus: Your greatest gift

Prayer Starter: Almighty God, thank You for giving me Your Love; it is who You are. Thank You for giving me Your Word; it is who You are. Thank You for giving Your Son; He is who You are. And thank You for creating me in Your image and equipping me with good and perfect gifts and talents that can minister to my personal needs and the needs of others. I surrender my most valuable gift to You, the Gift of who I am. Use me now in Your service to build Your Kingdom

_____

_____

_____

_____

_____

_____

_____

_____

In Jesus' name I pray. Amen, amen, and amen!

᙮

Do you know God did not give you anything just for you? Have you experienced the joy of giving yourself away?

Give who you are: Listen to what the Spirit says about it, and record what you hear.

_____

_____

_____

_____

_____

_____

_____

_____

_____

_____

_____

_____

_____

_____

_____

_____

_____

_____

_____

_____

_____

Date: _____

THE POWER OF THE HUMAN VOICE

"Words kill, words give life;
  they're either poison or fruit—you choose."

PROVERBS 18:21 (MSG)

WHAT A CHOICE, life or death; fruit or poison! The power of the human voice is unquestionable. How are you using your voice? People remember what—positive and negative—you say to them for a lifetime in many cases.

One day I picked my beautiful, chocolate niece, Walleisha, up from school. The first thing she said to me is, "Auntie, the kids call me black," and it was apparent she was not happy. She needed fruit for thought, and I chose to give it to her. My response was, "You are a pretty little black girl." Those words overpowered the poisonous words the kids said from that day to this. She is confidently living in her chocolate skin, proudly. As a life coach and minister, I realize the power of my voice can literally save a life. A young lady came into my life with issues that were causing her to have suicidal thoughts. It was a humbling experience when God used my voice to speak His Word, words of affirmation, encouragement, at times, words of correction, and love to talk her down off the wall.

How are you using your voice? Maya Angelou said, "Words mean more than what is set down on paper. It takes the *human voice* to infuse them with deeper meaning."

Be aware of the power of your voice and speak life-giving words of encouragement, affirmation, and love.

❧

Prayer Focus: Speaking live

Prayer Starter: Most Gracious Heavenly Father, there are times when I may not know what to say. Thank you for Logos, Your written Word, and the voice You gave me to speak those life-giving words to those I encounter, and yes, even to myself. Encouraging words: "You are more than a conquer," "Be strong and courageous," "By His stripes, you are healed." Holy Spirit, speak to and through me practical, meaningful words that will carry people through the challenges of life

_____

_____

_____

_____

_____

_____

In Jesus' name I pray. Amen, amen, and amen!

❧

Do you think before you speak? How are you using your voice?

The power of the human voice: Listen to what the Spirit says about it, and record what you hear.

_____

_____

_____

_____

_____

_____

_____

_____

_____

_____

_____

_____

_____

_____

_____

_____

_____

_____

_____

Date: _____

THE RECOVERY

"Therefore, I remind you to rekindle the gift of God that is in you through the laying on of my hands."

2 TIMOTHY 1:6 (CSB)

HAVE YOU EVER lost something, forgot you had something, or put something down and later recovered it? How did it make you feel?

I love telling the story of my daughter's recovery of her life's purpose. When she was twelve years of age, we knew Trellis was a teacher and she knew that she was a teacher. We signed for her to work in the church nursery. She loved teaching her cousins, anybody's children. Teaching was her purpose.

During her high school years, she put a mask on teaching and focused on careers that would enable her to make more money than Education. She received scholarships and a promise from the dean of the business school at North Carolina A & T University that he would place her in a Fortune-500 company upon graduation. It sounded good, but after two years with a 3.8 GPA, the recovery of her purpose began. She found herself rekindling God's gift within. Trellis confessed her calling to be a teacher. She transferred to Clark Atlanta University and majored in education. The rest is history; Dr. Trellis Davis serves as an assistant principal while passionately "fanning into flames" other God-given gifts.

Unmask who you are, professionally, spiritually, or otherwise, stir up your God-given gifts and let your recovery begin.

❧

Prayer Focus: Unmasking your purpose

Prayer Starter: Heavenly Father, thank You for Your prevailing purpose for my life. Holy Spirit, thank you for guiding me through the recovery of my gifts and purpose. Enable me to use them to the glory of God

_____

_____

_____

_____

_____

_____

_____

In Jesus' name I pray. Amen, amen, and amen!

∽

Do you have within yourself gifts and talents lying dormant? Can you imagine what it would be like to stir them up?

The recovery: Listen to what the Spirit says about it, and record what you hear.

_____

_____

_____

_____

_____

_____

_____

_____

_____

_____

_____

_____

_____

_____

_____

_____

_____

_____

Date: _____

SELF-DISCOVERY

"We all, with unveiled faces, are looking as in a mirror at the glory of the Lord and are being transformed into the same image from glory to glory; this is from the Lord who is the Spirit."

2 Corinthians 3:18 (CSB)

SELF-DISCOVERY CAN BE enlightening, frightening, exciting, and, yes, it can be profitable.

And so it is with my nephew. He honestly did not know about his genetic intelligence. He did not see his family connection relating to his thirst for knowledge, business acumen, and why his son was so gifted and smart. He saw the phrase "I am because you are" from the perspective of being a hard worker only.

Discovery time. I told him how smart his dad was, and among other things, I told him about the business acumen of his great-granddad, and he said, "Aunt B, I didn't know." I suggested he get to know his dad better. By discovering things about his great-granddad, stuff about his dad beyond the fact he was a hard worker who would give you the shirt off his back, Warren unveiled more about who he and his son are and who his daughter is (quite the businesswoman). Most importantly, Warren is discovering that he is being transformed in the image of Christ as he focuses on being who he was born to be and doing what God created him to do. The unmasking for my beloved nephew has been enlightening, sometimes frightening, exciting, and to God be the glory, profitable.

Are you ready for the unmasking of who you already are? Discover who you are so that you can enjoy an abundant life.

❦

Prayer Focus: Self-discovery

Prayer Starter: Almighty God, thank you for creating me in your image. Thank you for who I am in the natural and the spiritual

_____

_____

_____

_____

_____

_____

_____

In Jesus' name I pray. Amen, amen, and amen!

⊷

Do you know all there is to know about who you are? Have you ever done something and thought, "That is not like me?"

Self-discovery by unmasking: Listen to what the Spirit says about it, and record what you hear.

_____

_____

_____

_____

_____

_____

_____

_____

_____

_____

_____

_____

_____

_____

_____

_____

_____

_____

_____

_____

_____

_____

Date: _____

SILENCE, PLEASE

"Then they sat on the ground with him for seven days and nights. No one said a word to Job, for they saw that his suffering was too great for words."

JOB 2:13 (NLT)

THERE ARE TIMES when it is best to be quiet. Job experienced tremendous loss, including all his children. Three friends came to "sympathize with him and comfort him," and a remarkable thing happened.

After weeping for their friend, Job, they sat on the ground with him for seven days and nights in silence. After then, Job did something he needed to do for his emotional health. He opened up and started talking: "I cannot relax or be calm; I have no rest for turmoil has come." Have you or someone you know ever been where Job was?

Early in ministry training and experience, I learned about the power of silence. The next time you do a home or hospital visit or just hanging out with a friend who is experiencing challenges of any kind, consider giving them your silent presence. Allow them to do something that is emotionally healthy, open up and start talking. Silence, please.

❧

Prayer Focus: The power and presence of silence

Prayer Starter: God of mercy, God of grace, thank you for setting an example for us to follow. Thank you for always listening to our spoken and unspoken words. As you are a blessing to us, make us a blessing to others by enabling us to be quiet and allow others to speak when they need to talk

_____

_____

_____

_____

_____

_____

_____

_____

In the name of Jesus I pray. Amen, amen, and amen.

ॐ

Don't you love it when a friend understands your need for their presence and nothing else?

Silence, please: Listen to what the Spirit says about it, and record what you hear.

_____

_____

_____

_____

_____

_____

_____

_____

_____

_____

_____

_____

_____

_____

_____

_____

_____

Date: _____

TEACH THEM WELL

"Train up a child in the way he should go;
even when he is old he will not depart from it."

PROVERBS 22:6–8 ENGLISH STANDARD VERSION

I AM A baby boomer, and when I was growing up in South Georgia, it was a given that parents were a child's first teacher. It was also a given that the first lessons parents taught their children were straight out of the Bible. Among those lessons were the prayer Jesus taught His disciples, the Lord's prayer. Also, the grace or blessing food, and Bible verses—Jesus Wept; The Lord Is My Shepherd. I Shall Not Want; God Is Love—that you were expected to know and say at the dinner table, in Sunday school, or whenever asked.

They took their responsibility to "train up a child in the way they should go" seriously. Teaching children to love everybody, respect everybody (especially "old folk"), teach them to share, behave, speak to people, say thank you, and much more was a natural way of life. The parents desired to "teach them well," so they could survive and thrive in life.

Young parents, may I encourage you to consider teaching your children lessons that will sustain them as they face the challenges in life? Teach them well, straight out of the Bible. You will be glad you did.

Prayer Focus: Teaching children to pray and how to pray

Prayer Starter: Our Father who are in heaven, hallowed be Thy name. Let Thy kingdom come. Let Thy will be done in earth, in me, in my children as it is in heaven

_____

_____

_____

_____

_____

_____

_____

In Jesus' name I pray. Amen, amen, and amen!

౸

How necessary is a child's home training? Will it make a difference in the long term?

Teach them well: Listen to what the Spirit says about it, and record what you hear.

_____

_____

_____

_____

_____

_____

_____

_____

_____

_____

_____

_____

_____

_____

_____

_____

_____

_____

_____

Date: _____

EXCELLENCE: A MATTER OF THE HEART

"Whatever you do, work at it with all your heart, as working for the Lord, not for human masters, since you know that you will receive an inheritance from the Lord as a reward. It is the Lord Christ you are serving."

COLOSSIANS 3:23-24 (NIV)

ARE YOU WORKING your heart out? If so, is it for the next promotion, to impress or make someone proud of you? None of that is bad necessarily. But consider Daniel, whose life was an Old Testament demonstration of Paul's message in Colossians 3:23–24. Daniel was known for his spirit of excellence. Even the King knew that Daniel had a heart for God, and whatever he did, Daniel did it wholeheartedly to please God, not the king or his peers. And yes, Daniel knew that the reward he desired would come from the Lord.

Warning: Daniel's peers were intimidated by his spirit of excellence. They did not understand that it was not about him trying to be better. You may experience the same reaction from your peers.

Excellence is a matter of the heart. Put your heart in what you do and live out the Lord's purpose for your life, and you, like Daniel, will receive recognition, promotion, favor, and provision from those God ordained to be a blessing to you.

❧

Prayer Focus: Heart for God

Prayer Starter: All-Knowing Heavenly Father, thank You for everything you deposited in me—gifts, talent, purpose, wisdom… I desire to please You by putting my whole heart into using everything You have given me for Your glory. Open the eyes of man's heart, so my spirit of excellence is seen as a blessing to my fellow man

_____

_____

_____

_____

_____

_____

_____

In Jesus' name. Amen, amen, and amen.

ᔍ

Why are you working so hard? Who are you focused on pleasing?

Excellence: A matter of the heart. Listen to what the Spirit says about it, and record what you hear.

_____

_____

_____

_____

_____

_____

_____

_____

_____

_____

_____

_____

_____

_____

_____

_____

_____

_____

_____

_____

Date: _____

WHAT IS IN YOUR HEART?

"After this, Jesus, knowing that all things were not accomplished that the Scripture might be fulfilled, said, 'I thirst.'"

JOHN 19:28 (NKJV)

ARE YOU THIRSTY? I am. The Greek definition of thirst in John 19:28 means to desire strongly or desire earnestly. When Jesus said, "I thirst," it was not because He wanted something to drink to satisfy the need of His natural body. Jesus was expressing His passionate desire to fulfill every prophecy in the Old Testament concerning His earthly journey.

Like Jesus, I thirst for the fulfillment of my purpose here on earth. My heart desires to die empty. I want to use every good and perfect gift and talent God gave me. What about you? Do you know what is in your heart? Do you thirst for the opportunity to stir up the gifts in you? Know this, no matter where you are on your journey, it is not too late to do it. Jesus was hanging on a cross, dying a natural death when He cried out, "I thirst." And that statement triggered the action needed to quench His thirst.

&

Prayer Focus: Fulfillment of the desires of your heart

Prayer Starter: Creator God, You and You alone know from beginning to end the script for my life. I pray the Holy Spirit will give me revelation knowledge of what it is and a burning desire to see it fulfilled. Thank You for this thirst, thank you for my gifts and talents

_____

_____

_____

_____

_____

_____

_____

In Jesus' name I pray. Amen, amen, and amen!

⟨⟩

Is your heart full of desire? What are those desires?

What is in your heart: Listen to what the Spirit says about it, and record what you hear.

_____

_____

_____

_____

_____

_____

_____

_____

_____

_____

_____

_____

_____

_____

_____

_____

_____

_____

Date: _____

FELLOWSHIP

"A new commandment I give to you, that you love one another; as I have loved you, that you also love one another. By this all will know that you are My disciples, if you have love for one another."

JOHN 13:3–35 (NKJV)

THROUGH STUDY, OBSERVATION, and experience, I have learned that fellowship among Christians is "one of the most powerful concepts in scripture" and that fellowship results in *mutual* love.

Reading about fellowship in my Bible dictionary was an enlightening source of knowledge. Observation of fellowship among my family, church, and community growing up was inspirational, and it has been an influence on my life.

One of my college professors strongly believes that in John 13:34–35, Jesus commanded and established the "Ministry of One Anothering" because it represents who He is and who we are in relationship to Him. Speaking from experience, fellowship, communion with God and man is like the air I breathe, and I cannot live without it. It brings me joy, laughter, peace, and it gives me strength when I am weak, and it keeps me in a close relationship with my Heavenly Father and man. I thank Christ Jesus for enabling me to create opportunities for family and brothers and sisters in Christ to experience the blessings of fellowship. Knowing that the result will be obedience to Jesus' command in John 13:34–35 is rewarding. Fellowship is the ship that keeps all other relationships going, and I cannot live without it. Can you?

Prayer Focus: Fellowship with God and man

Prayer Starter: Almighty God, what a joy it is to commune with you, talking and listening to you. And even feeling your presence keeps me going

_____

_____

_____

_____

_____

_____

_____

In Jesus' name I pray. Amen, amen, and amen!

❧

Did you know fellowship is the ship that builds and keeps all relationships growing strong? How do you get to know people without some level of fellowship? Is intimacy possible without fellowship?

Fellowship: Listen to what the Spirit says about it, and record what you hear.

_____

_____

_____

_____

_____

_____

_____

_____

_____

_____

_____

_____

_____

_____

_____

_____

_____

_____

_____

_____

Date: _____

LAUGHING OUT LOUD

IT NEVER CEASES to amaze me how God reveals me to me through the words of my friend and pastor, James Powers. We were at a leadership fellowship in Constance Arnold's home when I realized that he was laughing at my laugh. And then, Pastor said for all to hear, "Brendal is back." Was he explaining to everyone why I had been cracking up all evening? No. He recognized a sign of healing; I was laughing again, really laughing. It was no longer a forced laugh; it was spontaneous. I would just burst out laughing, and it felt good.

Yes, I was still a widow and single mother, but God's healing power manifested through my laughter. It is a blessing to have people in your life who know and care enough to journey with you from a broken spirit to laughing.

The Bible says laughter does good like a medicine. My twist, laughter *is* a medicine.

I am still laughing. My husband, Gerald, is an excellent dispenser. My prayer is that no matter what challenges come your way, you will find yourself joyfully laughing your way through life.

Do you laugh easily? How does it feel when you are laughing? And is it better when you laugh out loud?

Laughing out loud: Listen to what the Spirit says about it, and record what you hear.

_____

_____

_____

_____

_____

_____

_____

_____

_____

_____

_____

_____

_____

_____

_____

_____

_____

_____

Date: _____

JOY-FULL

"The Lord is my strength and shield.
   I trust him with all my heart.
He helps me, and my heart is filled with joy.
   I burst out in songs of thanksgiving."

PSALM 28:7 (NLT)

PEOPLE HAVE OFTEN wondered what makes me tick, what gives me the strength to smile when I suffer a significant loss or face challenges in life. The only way I can explain it is joy—the spiritual fruit—strengthens me. It will continually give you the strength to face trials and tribulations in life.

I was not happy when my first husband drowned and I became a widow, but I still had joy. I was displeased when counseling did not rescue my second marriage and I became a divorcee, but I still had a joyful spirit. I was not happy when my daughter faced severe health challenges and my hair was coming out, but I still had joy.

The source of my strength is not a wonder; it is the One I have put my trust in, the One who helps me and fills my heart with joy. Simply speaking, His Joy keeps me strong and of good courage. What about you? What is the reading on your joy-o-meter? I believe the Lord wants it to read "Joy-Full."

❧

Prayer Focus: Joy

Prayer Starter: Most gracious Heavenly Father, thank you for Your joy. The joy that gives me the strength to live, love, laugh, smile, and dance, no matter what comes my way. Your joy enables me to keep moving toward my destiny. By the power of the Holy Spirit, my joy-o-meter reading is Joy-Full. Thank you

_____

_____

_____

_____

_____

_____

_____

In Jesus' name I pray. Amen, amen, and amen.

∽

From where does your strength come? What enables you to get back up again, and again, and again?

Joy-full: Listen to what the Spirit says about it, and record what you hear.

_____

_____

_____

_____

_____

_____

_____

_____

_____

_____

_____

_____

_____

_____

_____

_____

_____

_____

_____

_____

_____

_____

Date: _____

I ♔ SMILE

"When they were discouraged, I smiled and that encouraged them and lightened their spirits."

(MSG)

"When I smiled at them, they could hardly believe it; their faces lit up, and their troubles took wing!"

JOB 29:24 (LIVING)

I SMILE ON purpose. "Intentionally and unintentionally, knowingly and unknowingly, happy or sad. I smile as easily as I breathe because one of my purposes in life is to bless and encourage with a smile. Through it all, the good times and bad, I smile because God created me to *be* a smile. To *God* be the glory, i ♔ SMILE!"

Those words came to me on January 30, 2019, as words of encouragement. As beautiful and warm as a smile is, there are times when some are not receptive to it. It bothers them, especially when they are going through challenges. They prefer to be greeted by a straight face instead. But God knows best. A smile lightens spirits; it lights up people's faces, and according to Job 29:24, believe it or not, it causes trouble to take wings. Praise God, that is why I smile, and that is a reason for you to bless and encourage people with the beautiful smile God gifted to you. The song says, "I know God is working, so I smile."

∽

Prayer Focus: The warmth, beauty, and power of a smile

Prayer Starter: Heavenly Father, thank you for gifting me with a smile. Thank you for the powerful ministry in a smile. Holy Spirit, thank you for living big in me even when I am not at my best, cause me to share a smile that encourages and warms the hearts of others. By faith, I know you are working in every situation and circumstance, so thank you for the gift of giving and receiving a smile in good times and challenging times

_____

_____

_____

_____

_____

_____

_____

In Jesus' name I pray. Amen, amen, and amen!

❧

What is in a smile? Have you thought about the impact your smile has on others?

i ♛ Smile: Listen to what the Spirit says about it, and record what you hear.

_____

_____

_____

_____

_____

_____

_____

_____

_____

_____

_____

_____

_____

_____

_____

_____

_____

_____

Date: _____

PRAYER

The anointing is on the prayer Jesus taught His disciples, including Christians, to pray. What a blessing it is that we need not struggle with how or what to pray. It is a pure prayer that recognizes and testifies to the omniscience and omnipotence of God, and it is available to us all. This prayer is complete, not a prayer starter; I encourage you to pray it often.

Matthew 6:9–13 New King James
In this manner, therefore, pray:
Our Father in heaven,
Hallowed be Your name.
Your kingdom come.
Your will be done
On earth, as *it is* in heaven.
Give us this day our daily bread.
And forgive us our debts,
As we forgive our debtors.
And do not lead us into temptation,
But deliver us from the evil one.
For Yours is the kingdom and the power and the glory forever.
Amen.

Have you ever been lost for words to pray? Don't be. The prayer above is a pure prayer—not too long, not too short. It is always in season and includes everything you need to say to Your Heavenly Father.

Prayer: Listen to what the Spirit says about it, and record what you hear.

_____

_____

_____

_____

_____

_____

_____

_____

_____

_____

_____

_____

_____

Date: _____

ABOUT THE AUTHOR

Brendal Bass Davis is a wife, mother, ordained minister, certified personal coach, teacher, and founder and leader of the Spirit of Excellence Ministry SOEM, Inc. Through her ministry with SOEM, Inc., she leads the Motivators Group. As a success evangelist, Brendal has a passion for inspiring individuals to be who they were born to be and do what they were created and gifted to do. She was born and raised in Thomasville, Georgia, and currently resides in Stonecrest, Georiga. *I Will Not Be Quiet About It* is her first book. To learn more about the SOEM ministry, please visit www.luv2inspire.net.

CPSIA information can be obtained
at www.ICGtesting.com
Printed in the USA
LVHW080824020821
694026LV00018B/841